GW00750838

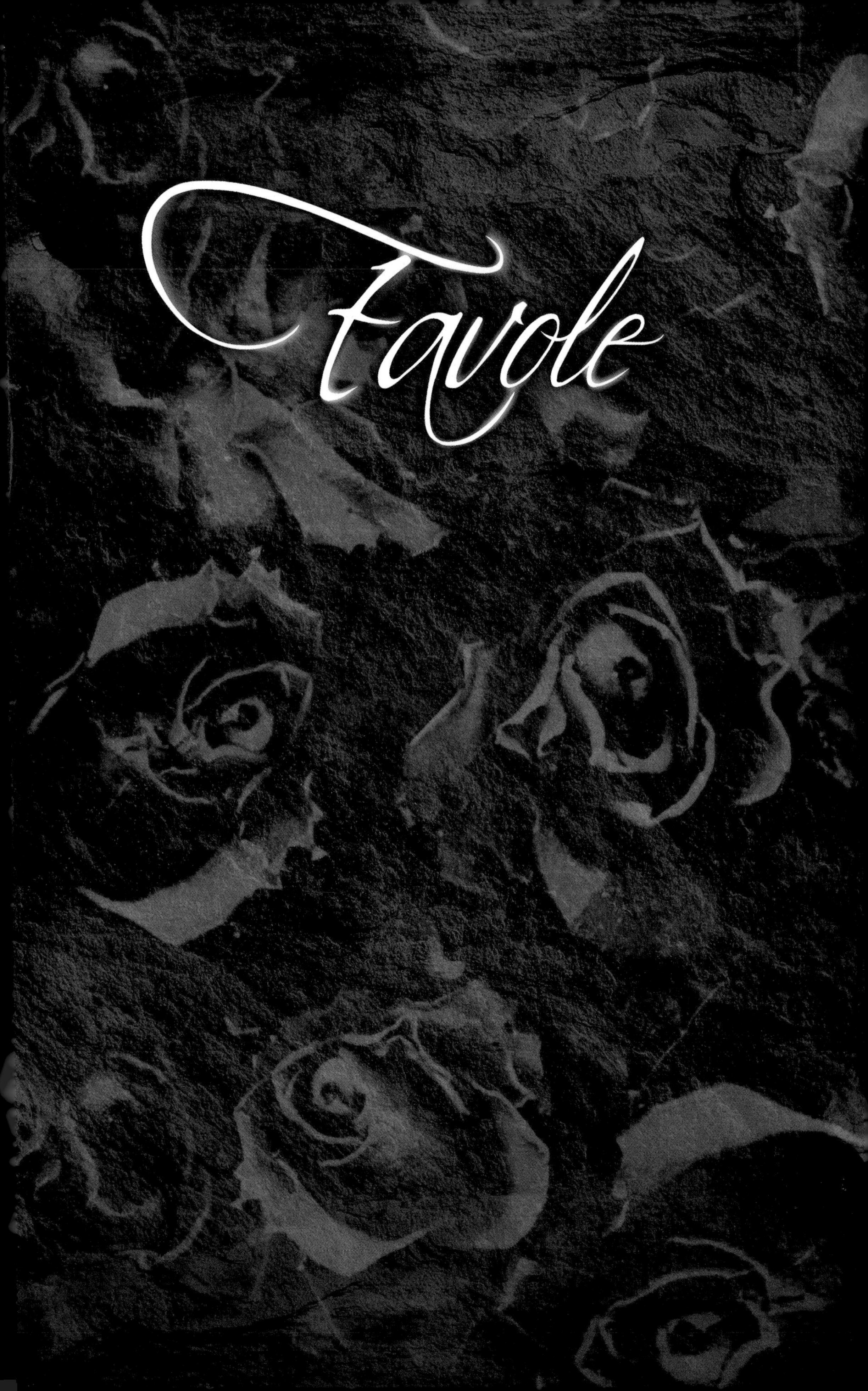
Favole

"Even in the dark
there was a light of some
kind, as there ever is over
snow, and it seemed as
though the snow flurries
and the wreath of mist
took shape as of women
with trailing garments."

Bram Stoker, Dracula

Remembrances of three cities: Verona, Venice and Genoa.
To my fathers.

FAVOLE BOOK ONE: STONE TEARS
ISBN 978-19324-13816
© Victoria Francés / represented by Norma Editorial
Published by Heavy Metal ®
100 North Village Avenue, Suite 12,
Rockville Centre NY 11570
Nothing may be reproduced in whole or
in part without the written permission
of the publisher
Printed in the China

Favole

1. Stone Tears

Victoria Francés

HEAVY METAL

I remain forever bewitched
by times past...

Somewhere in my memories, the pale women, awakened by longing, walked in the company of The Sorrowful and Forlorn amongst hundreds of cold, worn statues.

The immortal beat of my yearning had driven me through limitless mountains of dead leaves, barren winters, and legendary castles. On a murky, endless hall, I began my road. I ran through the darkness, traversing hundreds of antique vaults, nearly losing myself in the beauty of their languid gazes.

Not until then, had my ladies found their way to the forest, since prior they'd remained in a state of lethargy, surrounded by the walls of a thousand fortresses and dark mansions, tormented by grotesque beasts that dwelled in the dungeons of my dreams. But dreamlike remnants of their wilted existence will linger forever, those scenes sinking deeper and deeper in the fog, where the sun gets lost forever and the ruins of love remain standing beneath the violent sob of rains and storms.

The lamp that was lit to illuminate my darkness stopped giving its quivering glow, yielding to natural light…

Introduction

I can't remember… how I found the main entrance to the castle, and made my way out, 'cross the drawbridge and through the iron gates that guarded my chiaroscuro dreams. Only to find myself in the grove, where I've seen elves that seemed to smile upon me as I floated out on ponds of amber.

But beyond the forest, danger and sadness await, and of course, a thousand pleasures. I knew I was free when I looked around and millions of sounds and colours rose before me. The old stories returned to my mind and I recalled the laughter of the old witches, who flew on their brooms across the purple skies of my intimacy.

Cities I've yet to know await me, and I shall uncover the legends of the mysterious princes and the sounds of their immortal music.

If, at last, I finally know love, it will be in the arms of a dream-like vampire, drunk on that music, free of any fright.

Submerged in his warmth, smoothness, and seduction…

And my whispered name, Favole.

Victoria Francés

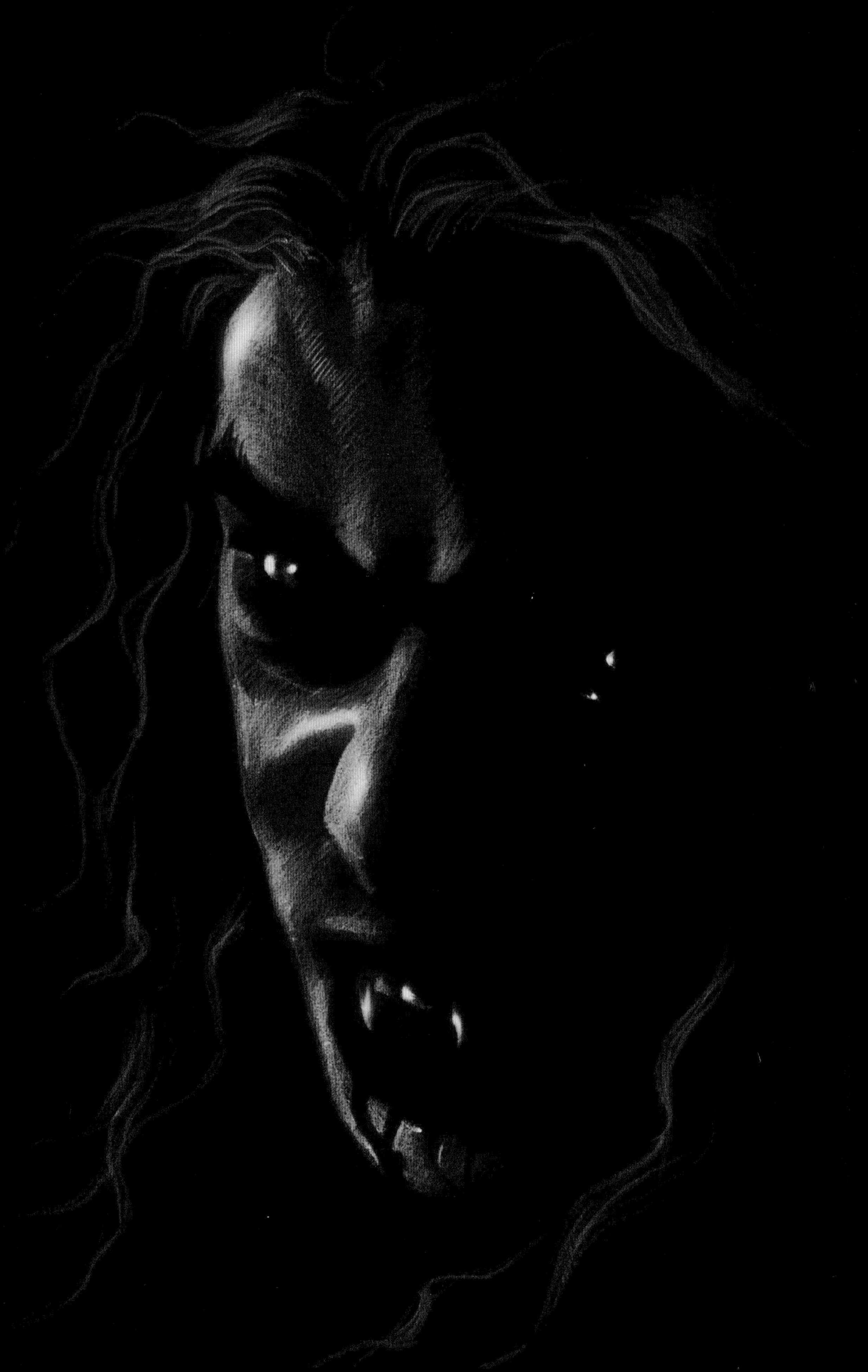

Prologue

Breathless, he took refuge in the darkest place in the fortress And contemplated the horizon...

The last time he had traversed those roads he knew —beyond the forest of the ill-fated grove-openings existed, made of tearstained white shrouds. And in each paradise, each atmosphere made of old portals by silent angels, forgotten memories were being written. Hiding in half-light, black tears slid down his ashen cheeks, sketching a languid smile.

He knew the faces of all the ladies he'd forced to wander beneath stormy skies. Of all the sinister princes, it was he who hid behind masks of horrendous beasts and kissed the cheeks of lush beauties. Stroking their breasts, he'd drained leagues of the rubies that flowed from their veins, as those dying maidens moaned of pleasure, leaking the dew of their tears.

Ezequiel... knight shrouded in darkness. The spirits asleep beneath sheets of dead leaves curse you! The gleaming light in your eyes longs to recite the litany of restless ladies... Countless wilted roses are crying for them!

Now, like ivy, undulating silhouettes rush to the loneliness of your empty bedchambers, keeping you company in the web of your memories, and at the end of remembrance, you know you will feel the ancient call to caress once again one of their purple manes.

Trapped in your unreality like a hidden specter in some abandoned bell tower... their lips like roses now drip the blood of times past...

"If thou wilt be mine, I shall make thee happier than God
Himself in His paradise. The angels themselves will be jealous of thee. Tear off that
funeral shroud in which thou art about to wrap thyself. I am Beauty, I am Youth,
I am Life. Come to me! Together we shall be Love."

Théophile Gautier, *Clarimonde*

Virgins
of the Lake

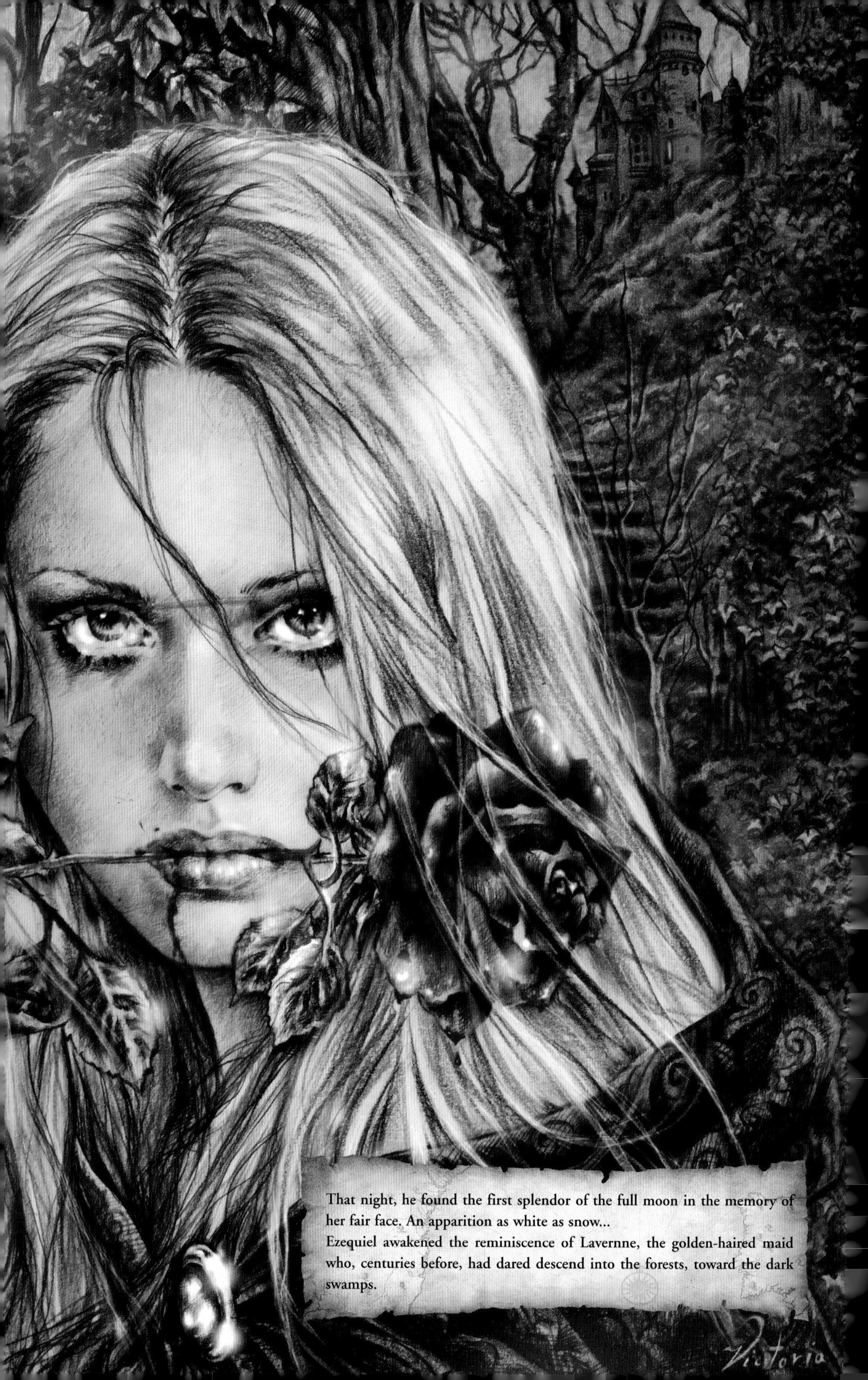
That night, he found the first splendor of the full moon in the memory of her fair face. An apparition as white as snow...
Ezequiel awakened the reminiscence of Lavernne, the golden-haired maid who, centuries before, had dared descend into the forests, toward the dark swamps.
Victoria

He remembered her livid glow whilst she gazed sky-
ward, bidding the stars farewell as dawn came…
Trembling, after envisioning death taking hold of her
father's body, Lavernne walked with tremulous spasms,
loosing herself a labyrinth of endless paths. Legend was
the old Crusades orphaned many young women coiled
in penury.

Stifling a vision, the old vampire mentally captured the
purity of that dying, tearful visage on the banks of a
pond. He soothed her wailing for life with a decisive
embrace, kissed her sorrow-laden veins, and left her
outstretched body to float out on the stillness of the
waters.

He imagines her now,
sprouting from the gloom
of the darkness.

In the coming days, they found her swollen body on a river's bank. No one knew what happened to her waxen, lifeless body. They say her golden hair had turned to white, and her blue lips retained a sweet smile.

"Lavernne..." Whispers of that name still issue from the lips of the undead. In the loneliness of his bedchambers, you can hear the music of an old clavichord commemorating the dance of her white hair. Never again would he visit that spirit ensnared in the waters, but the old, hunchbacked witches affirm that even today you can hear her sylph chants, emanating far off, from the deepest recess of the forest.

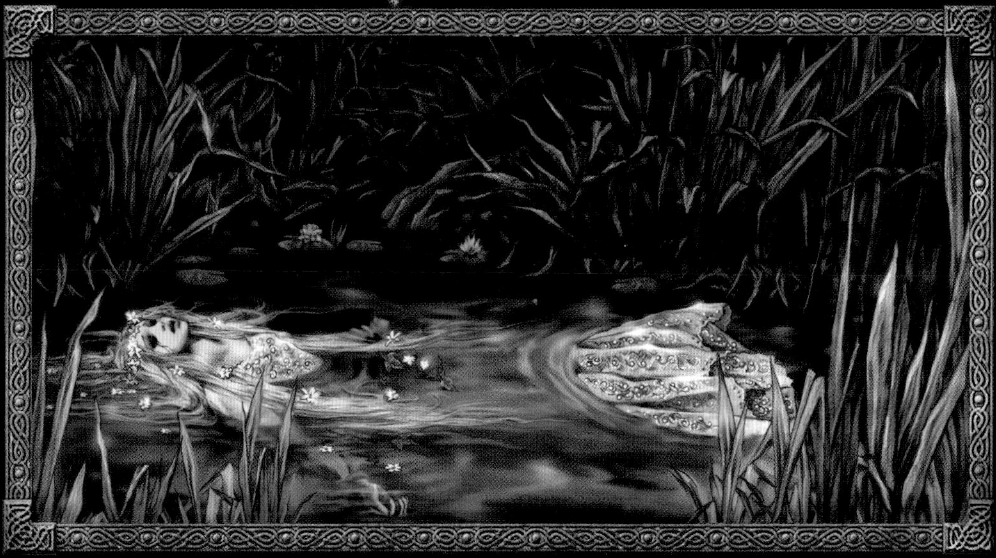

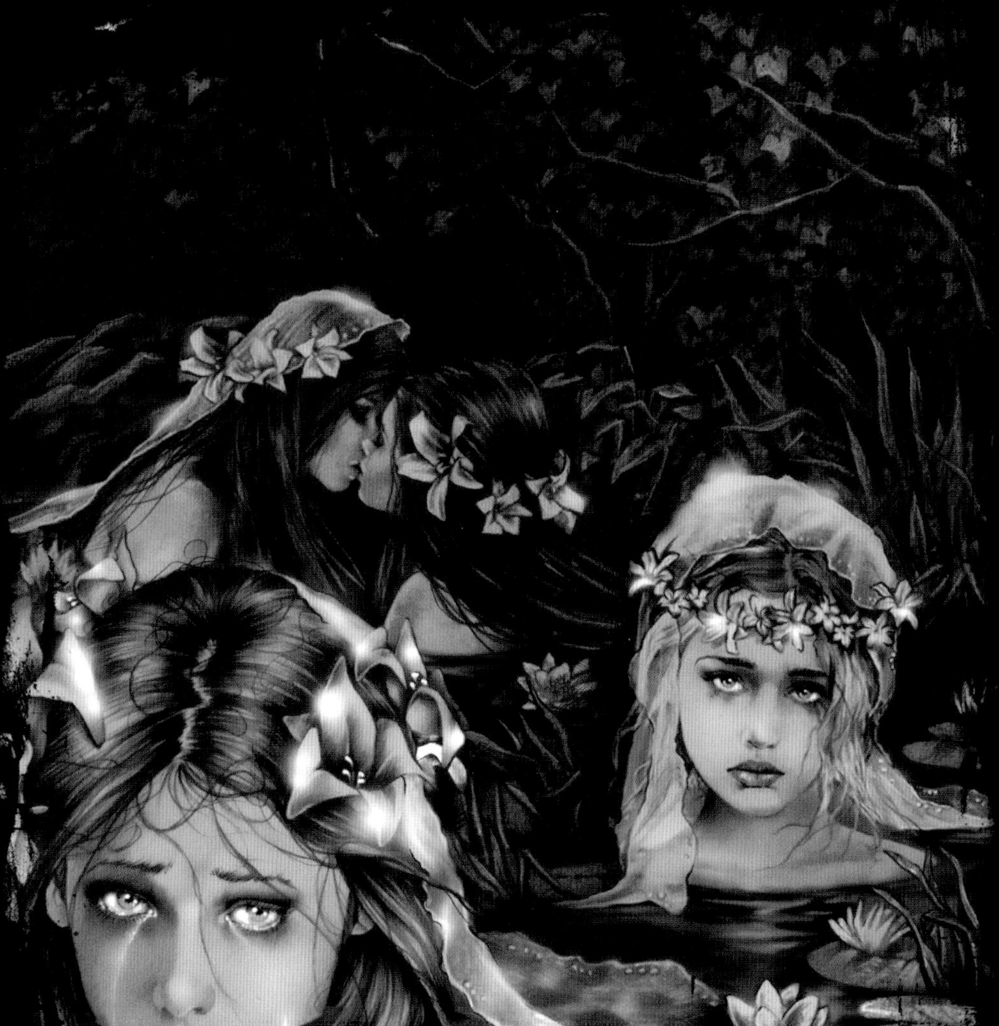

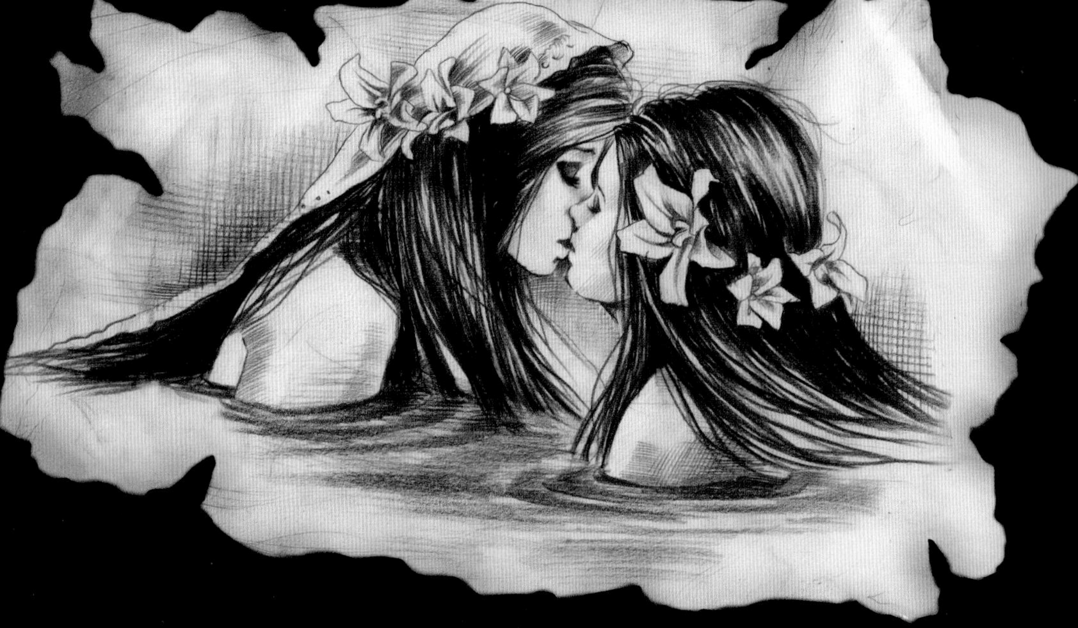

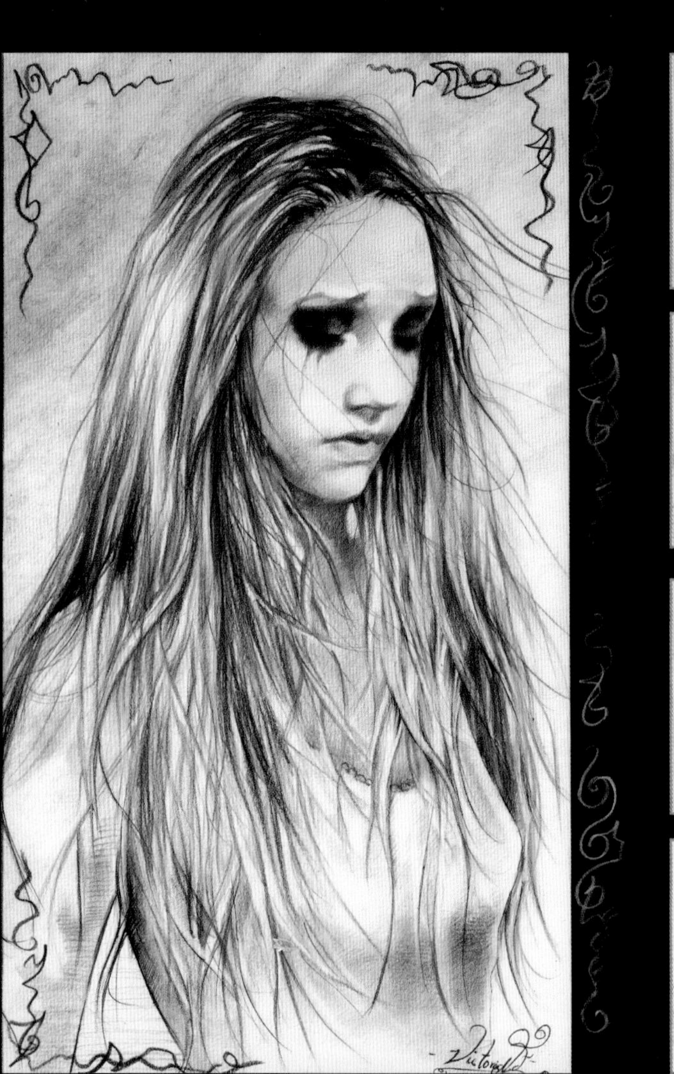

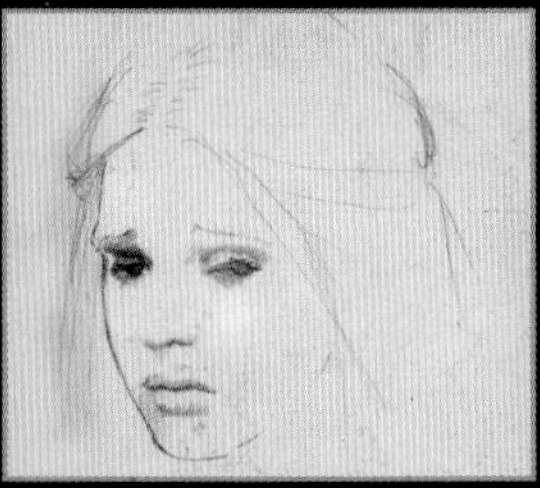

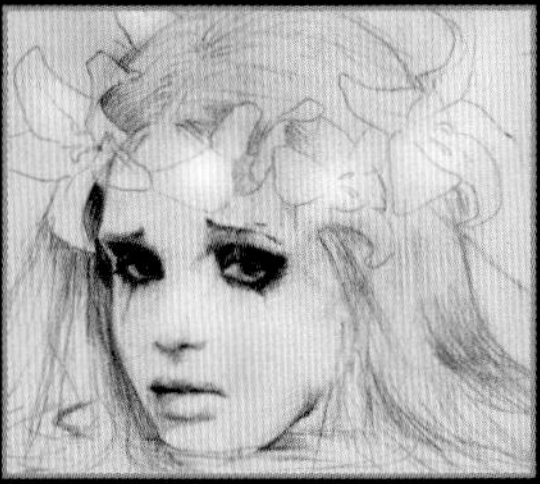

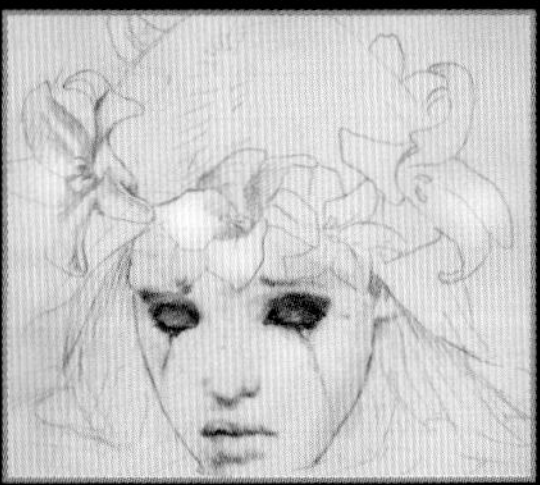

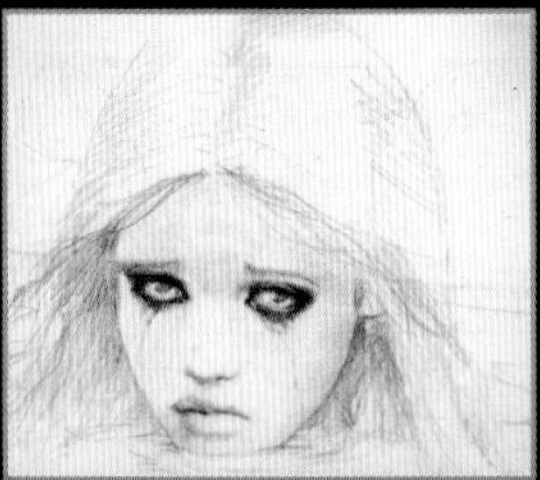

As though mystically entranced, thousands of girls, driven by the passion in their loins, leave their villages to listen to the culmination of Lavernne's melodies. All of them, orphaned from affection after their deaths, visit the beds where their fathers lay, and submerge then in the deepness of the pond, displaying the love they profess to their albino queen. In the court of submerged virgins, reigns the empress of that cloudy land, an Ophelia suffocated in mud, who long since ventured to cross the rivers, delirious in the mist.

*L*egions of innocent virgins sleep beside her; embracing one another amidst the fluid vegetation. Immaculate virgins who learn of lesbian love with damp caresses. They dream of discarding their chastity to discover the pleasures of flesh in a palace built of crystal towers. Crowned in their dementia, like angels from some mythic paradise, they wait for the frost...

... and then awaken, exhaling nervously among the foam and algae. They are the lovers of the moss, lavishly dressed and courted by doomed knights in rusted armor, escorted to an endless calendar of banquets and masked balls...

Illustrious, the albino deity questions the absent stares of frogs for the name of her life-less lover: that impious prince who extended her coverlets 'cross the diamond waters and kissed her frozen neck. But those phantasmagoric amphibians remain silent, despite her pleas, sheltering the shiver of their secret.

To shield herself from lack of love, she crowns her hair with wild flowers and dreams of being princess queen in her palace of mud and water… hoping eternally to embrace once more a father killed in wars past, longing to offer him her sharpened teeth in bloody kisses, so both might submerge together into the reign of winter waters. Beyond a swamp flooded with fog, the deceased princess continues thus appearing like a spectral nymph, at sunset, when the naked trees shun protection from the rain or when fall covers in ochre the deepness of that arcane river.

Somewhere in the palace of water, in the darkness, Lavernne still mourns for her orphanhood, purging her grief in that land of mud and crystal where once she wandered, cloaked in her insanity.

Where a prince abandoned her body
to the embrace of nebulous waters...

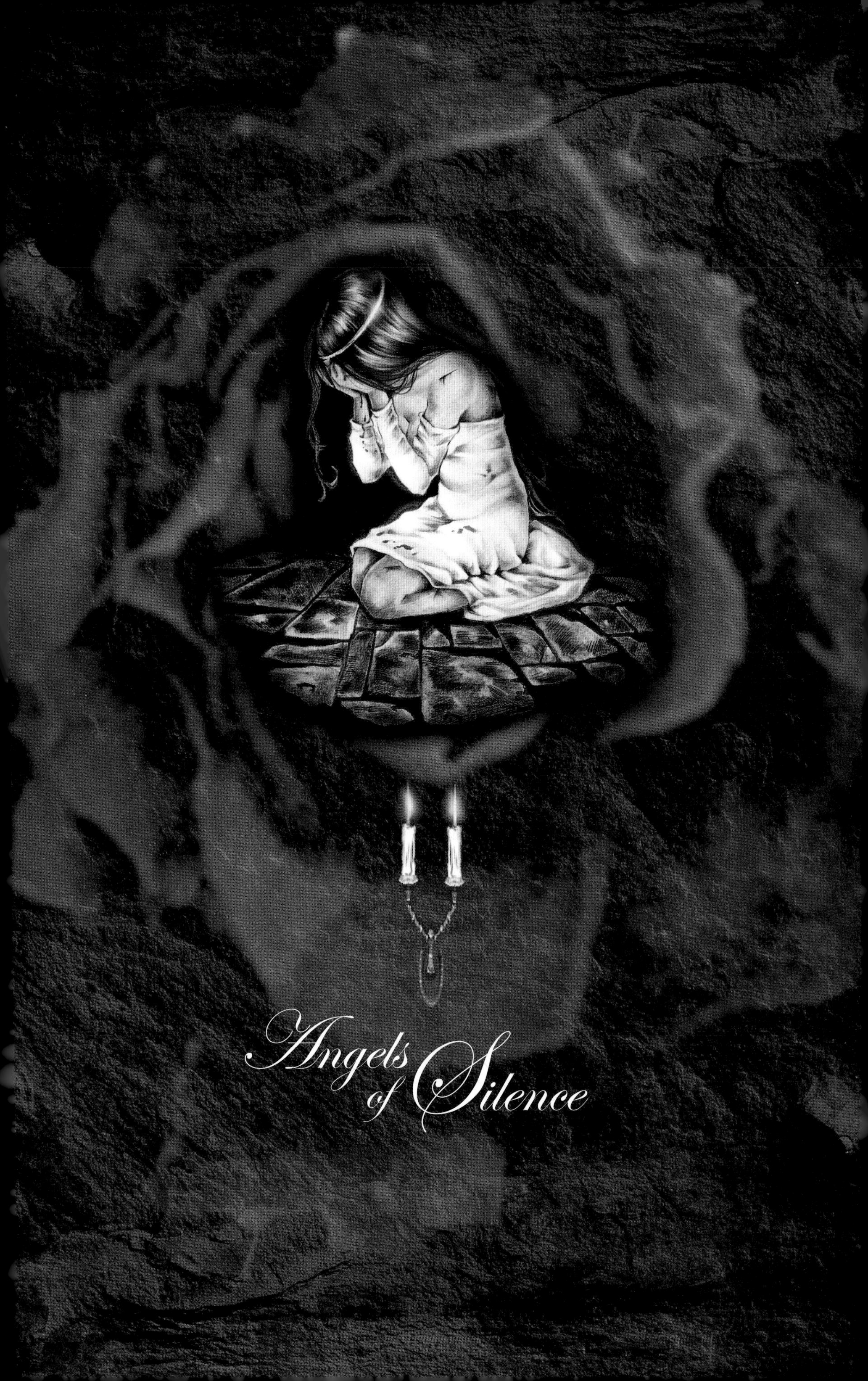
Angels of Silence

Marquise loved to contemplate those stony eyes beneath the faint light of an oil lamp...
When the memory of murky marshes subside, the worn-looking knight urged the years
flow on through memory's cache to revisit Marquise, the Romanian princess of his
forefathers. From her he'd learned the language of violins, overflowing his imagination
with the turmoil of artistic inspiration and his lover for life.

Her walk was that of an idealist at heart – paths of tombstones opened before her, deserting those that lay beneath their epitaphs, accompanied always by the sound of breeze exhaling with extreme languidness from a nearby forest's tree. Ezequiel imagined passing his fingers across the rough texture of the stone and for an instant understood the strange passion Marquise had once felt for an idyllic angel made of stone.

Since her childhood, the young princess had been dazzled by that statue's sweet smile and those wings, broken by time, which seemed to share her innocence among the shadows of that city of the dead.

The love for that lifeless cherub amounted to so much that, with the passage of time, the desire to sculpt was born in her, a wish to reconstruct his destroyed wings and to rouse him with music unheard through the rhythms of her crimson violin. She would have tried anything to endow with life the stony figure who then so eclipsed her heart. The dark lover covertly observed her artistic delirium for years until, one night, he came to share her aspirations beneath the shadow of the stone figure. Ezequiel listened intently to the young woman who had engorged his own imagination while she begged how she might bring to life that sublime, silent angel. He respected her innocence but for a few moments… and then flew forth as a vampire would, forever unsatiated, thrashing his wings and leaving behind the dying girl, laying mournfully beautiful at the sculpture's feet.

Since then, and to this day, the sweet maiden can see his face at sunset, in a faraway castle where she walks past hundreds of imposing walls, chanting songs in the silent corridors of his great fortress. Amidst the webs of her past, she remembers the faces of all the ladies portrayed with their languid looks, the oldness of the old knights against the brilliant splendor of their silver armor. Ezequiel always knew, even after her death, she would revert to her old passions, her musical gift, her incessant strolling, alone and invisible, whilst all the world slept.

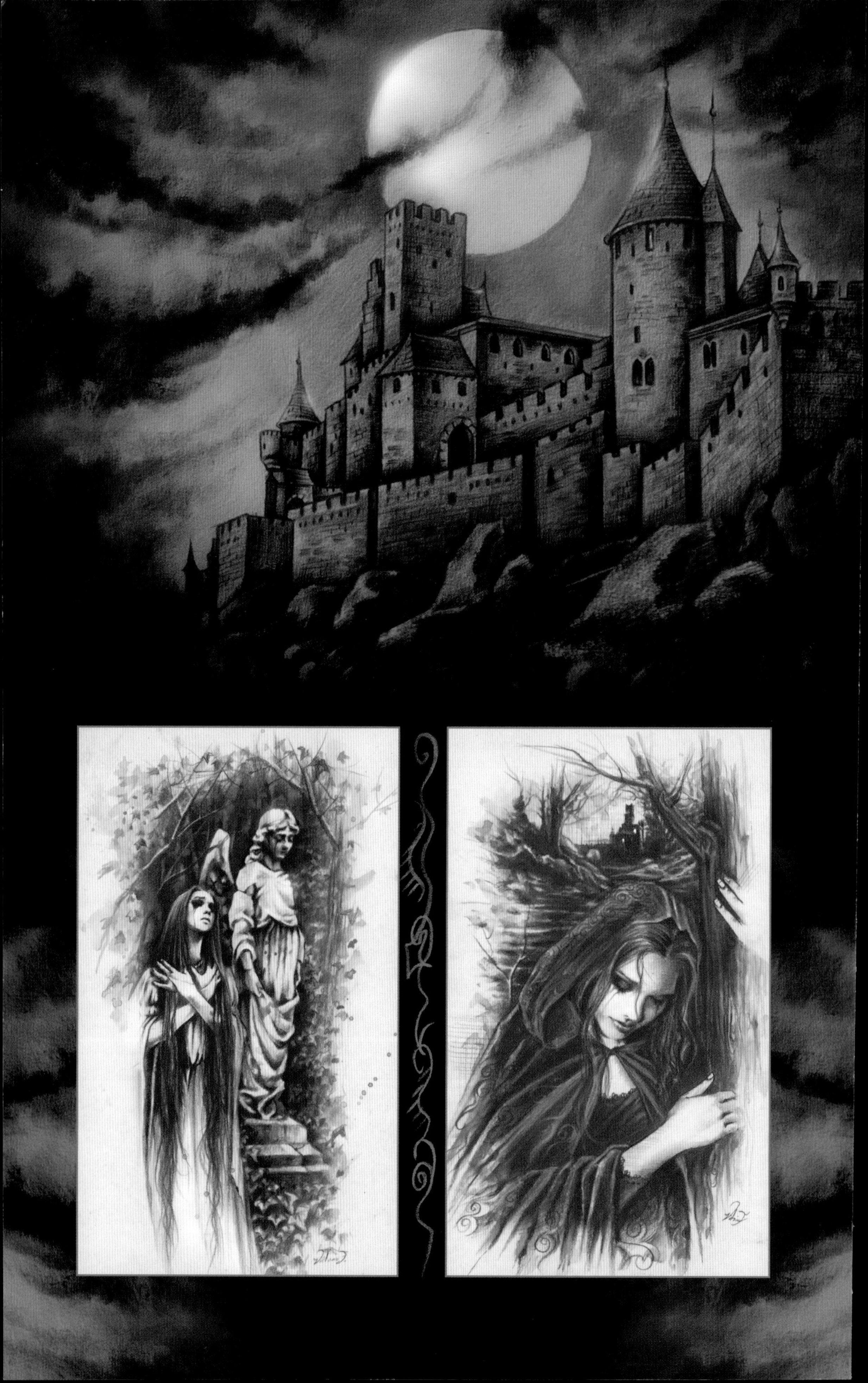

For centuries, her sleep has been guarded by a beautiful, marble cherub, whose cold wings tear her dress when she awakens to contemplate the passage of time.

The smiling angel whispers her name with a rhythmic tremor, and she comes to feel as dead as he is.

Many years have passed since they contracted nuptials, and from the cold jugular of the loved one the dream of blood is drunk, plunging her into a somnambulistic fantasy in which they consummate with an unbridled passion.

For some time, Ezequiel observed the gargoyle with horrendous eyes, raised impetuous, controlling the horizon. The white maiden left her mark between the rickety claws of time and mold, where long ago she lifted the shroud that covered her breasts, and upon which rough surface she dug her nails, searching for signs of life, long before her ramble toward the castle had begun.

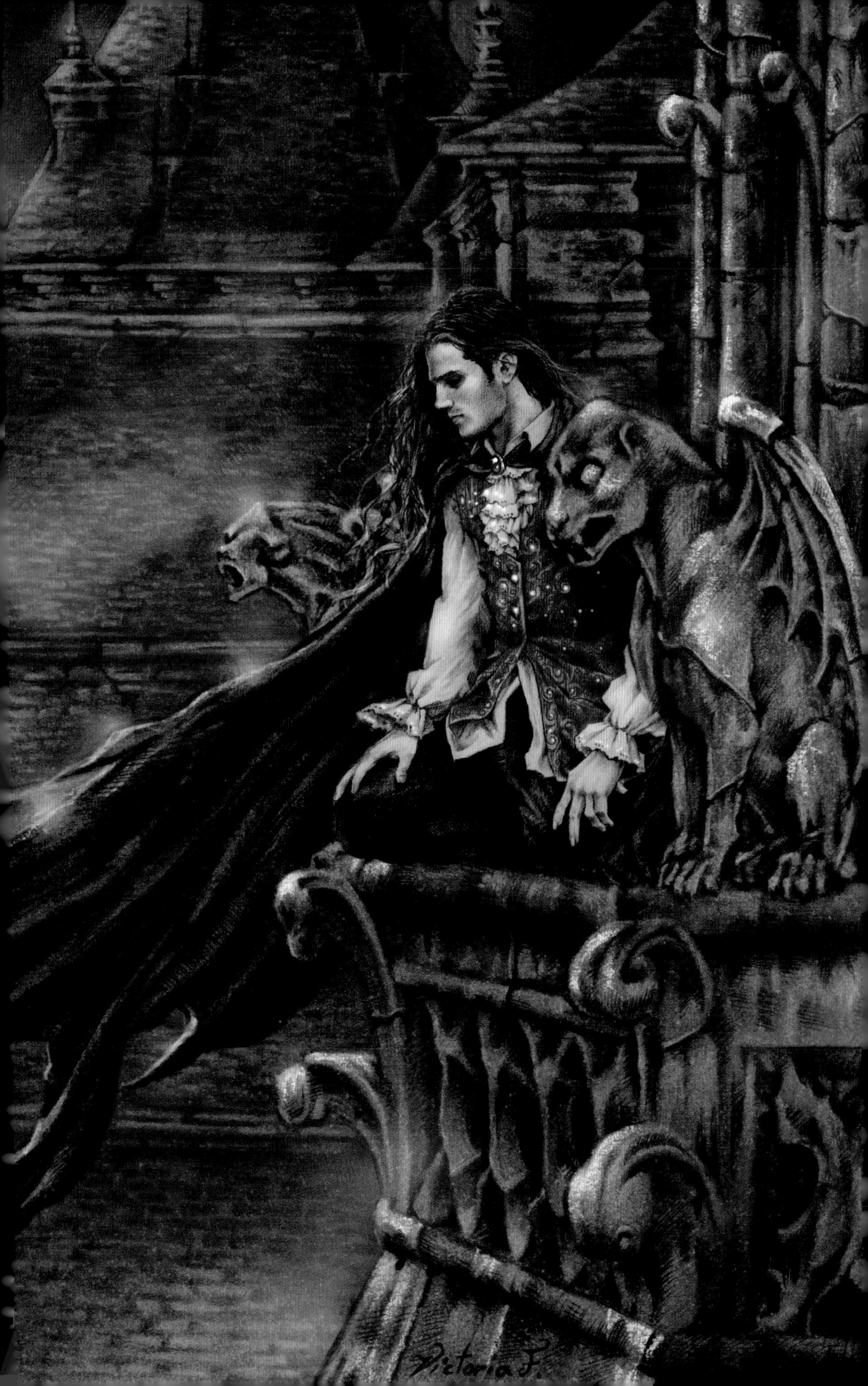
Victoria F.

Like a soprano lost in memory, she will continue singing melodies of pagan songs, behind the walls of a parlor covered in dust, there, in the halls flooded by forgotten ancestors in rusted armor. She will never lose the love for her artistic gift. What's more, she will always dance among the ivy, bowing her red violin, playing tribute for her stone lover.

The princess of fairy tales exists like a transient fire in the reality of that holy ground.

No prince of death came to visit her ever again. None kissed her lifeless remains to resuscitate her body as it lay scattered in the leafage.

Her dark father never forgets her... His daughter will be the light that guides the walk of all the girls who died in the hands of evil stepmothers, of all the witches who in their misfortune were judged and burned. She is the specter of the castle, forever beautiful, eternal...

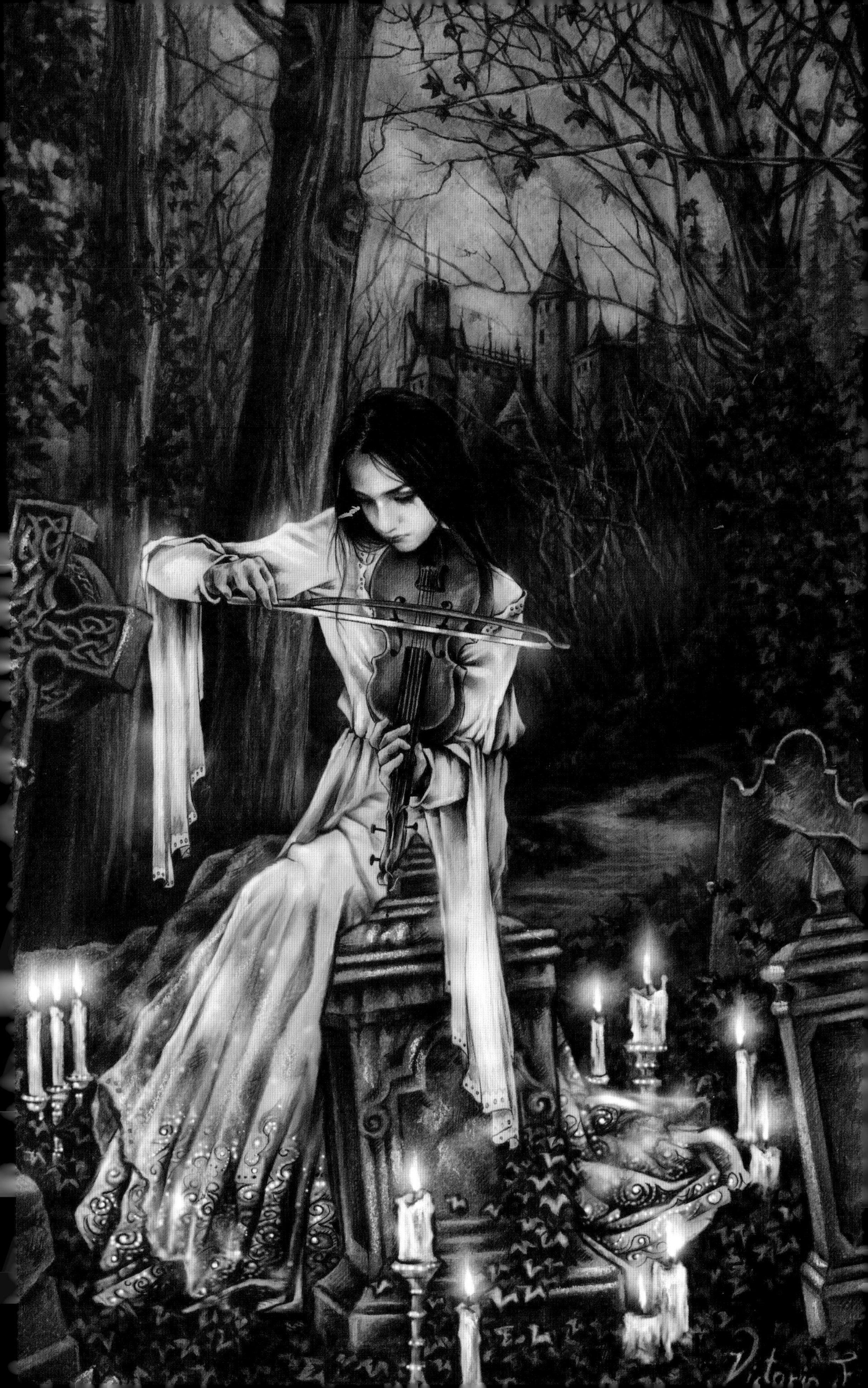

In the sound of violins, her smile
remains engraved. Her sibylline image
among fog and breeze.

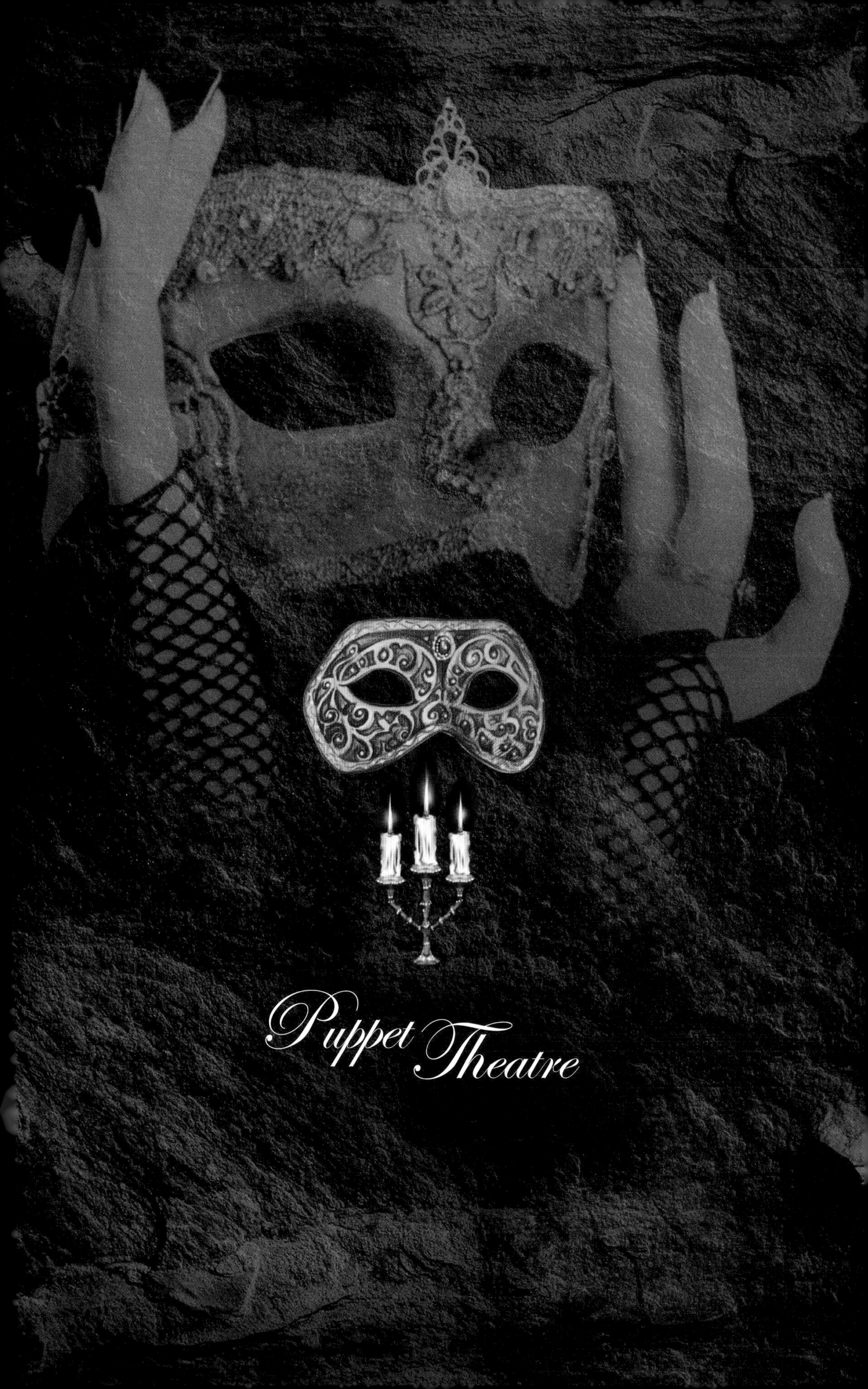
Puppet Theatre

In those rooms, you could feel the weight of the night, oozing centuries of yearnings, as sure as gusts of wind blew the wavering light of the candelabras...

For centuries he lived only with the memories of his two daughters, lost among the dusty lines of legends… but there were moments when the ephemeral fragrance of mahogany hair flooded the small, dark chamber.

The vampire moved away from the window and curled up on the bed, where he began to evoke the fascination he felt for the face that would mark him for the rest of his existence. "...Favole..." Her name echoed everywhere in the castle, hammering the sad monarch's frozen heart. Dressed in mourning, he allowed himself to drift to his deepest nostalgic abyss, and in his memory he lighted upon the hurtful remembrance of that lady, crying tears of blood for the loss of his most beloved jewel...

He conjured her image as it was, centuries ago, in the loneliness of a milky landscape where he'd first glimpsed her body, shivering in the drowsiness of a winter wind.

He remembered her as if it were yesterday, her body frozen in snow, grappled up in the caress of the beautiful white werewolves.

It was he who preserved her innocence from a cold death, he who cradled her in his arms inside his carriage and brought her to the castle, protecting thus the beauty of her tedious lethargy. In the quiet of a peaceful chamber, as he contemplated her sleeping face, it was easy to discern her heritage. He drew forth images of an Italian city, where gondolas strolled smoothly on the dark canals.

And it was her dormant heart that expressed her passion for the theatre, in Venice. He saw alleys where she'd set her puppet theatre, saw her dressed in the colours of a smiling jester, and watched her mend the small garments that her grinning puppets wore.

After sunset, the adoring vampire offered her his castle, and by midnight celebrated a ghoulish masquerade in her honor, with melodies that awoke the copper-haired maiden from her weary slumber. Ezequiel will never forgot her expression –alive and exalted- in those early hours populated with a host of undulating specters...

Next to the handsome knight cloaked in nocturnal galas, she danced in the infinity of the night, surrounded by the curious expectations of all the other strange guests in that sinister court.

Never did a nocturnal being have such feelings for a living being. She, who should have been destined to be the banquet of the immortals, slept that night next to Ezequiel's cold body, submerged in the frozen caress of death. More than one hundred moons passed before Favole knew of the eternal condemnation that weighed on the creature that saved her life. Captivated by the immortal specter, she wished to share his misfortune, to drink eternally his ill-fated sentence...

He remembered her last stormy sunrise like it was yesterday. That candor of her pleading, her longing, and his restrained wish to destroy everything in the bedchamber, this same bedchamber, steeped with his filth. A helpless sob escaped the sinister prince, still he kept on evoking his misery, remembering and repenting for the rage that he'd left as he'd rejected her pleas, unwilling to condemn her body to such putrid existence.

He had not allowed the temptation of love to stand in the way of his fury. He expelled the maiden from his castle, restraining his instinctual desire to give her eternal death...

Favole fled, leaving the dark prince and his grotesque court far behind. Sobbing, she crossed a thousand different cities, always haunted by the blasphemous love she's felt within the infinite walls of his fortress.

She never imagined that her ship would one day dock in Genoa, a city where her muddled memories suddenly made sense, and where she dreams of someday crossing the sea again to walk the land of ghosts that never rest. But years of absence and madness afflicted the face of the Queen of the banished.

"Favole..." the ghosts of her macabre puppets murmured in unison. Without delay, she threw herself into Genoa's sea, to suffocate her life in the stormy waves...

Who doesn't recall her, smiling at her own wilted existence and then vanishing under the water, trapped like a hunchback in a bell tower? Favole, confidante to the unfortunate and the lame, those who failed to find their place in this world. Daughter of Quasimodo. Beautiful sirens accompanied the maiden in her misfortune and buried her drowned body in the lands of Neptune's valley. In the deceased's last slumber, the king of the seas forced Favole to wander forever in the dreams of the damned and traced an insurmountable wall between the two lovers to keep them forever apart, in their separate worlds...

Now, far from her watery tomb, she glows translucent in her carriage decked with diamonds, crossing frozen mountain peaks, dressed in sumptuous clothes and wearing crystal slippers affixed with sapphires.

There is no night in which the legendary vampire doesn't evoke in his dreams the return of Favole to his baroque parlors, to spin dances to the immortal music. But she hides no longer behind the pearls of his legions of long-nosed masks. Now she runs bravely through the weeds of Verona's forests and buries herself playfully under the leaves to dream with the dwellers in fairy tales. She tells her faraway lover that, when she was a child, she played with the rats in the streets, and they sweetly caressed her, because they were the only ones that truly learned to love her.

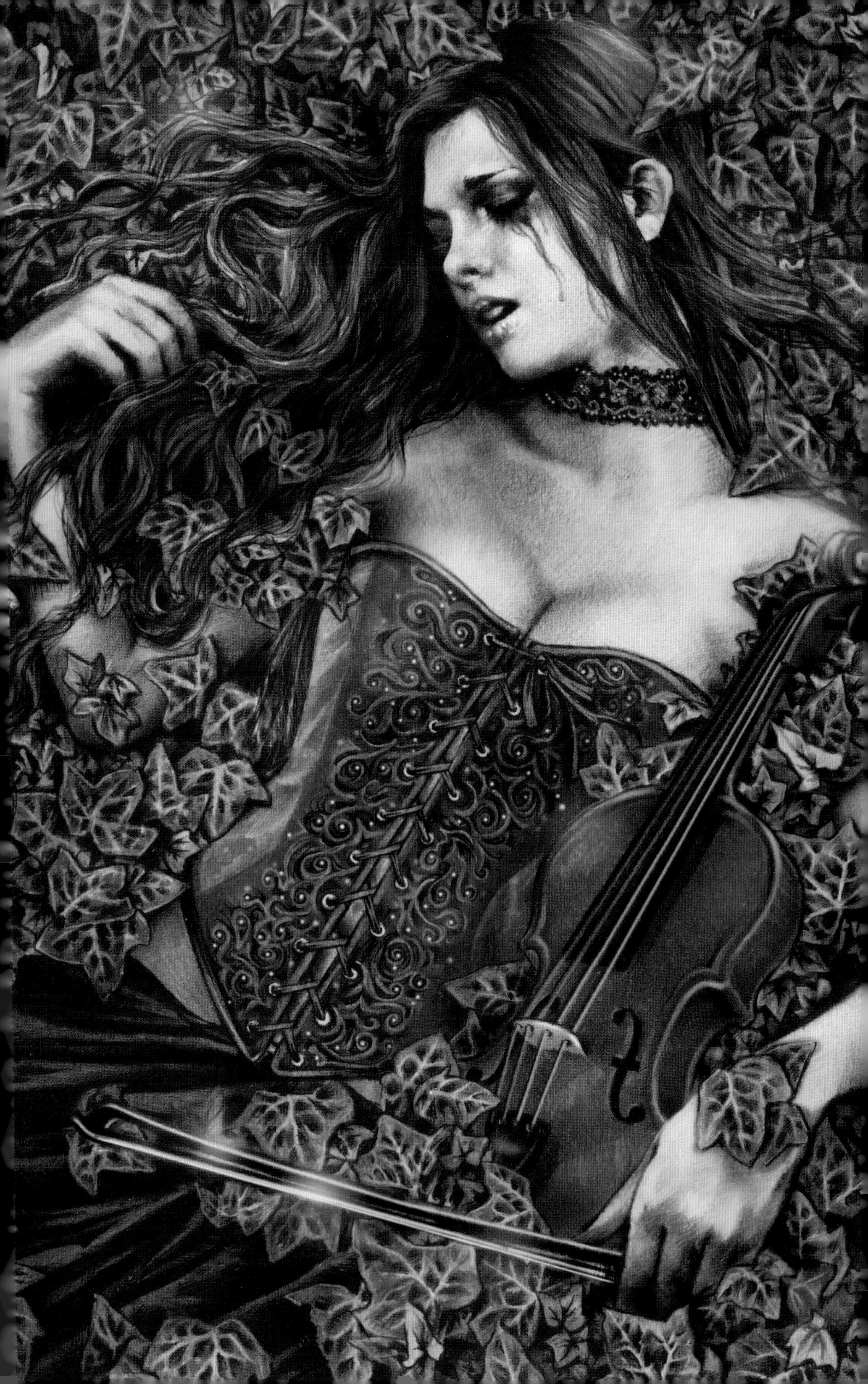

Since then, a puppet theater has closed its act, yielding to a dance of music and color. The mysterious gaze of the masked dancers, who fell in love with Cinderella in her Venetian palace, will always come back to her memory.

Under the vaults of infinite halls, she will now continue her road... "I will wait for you in Genoa, lover of my imagination..."

As she repeats these words, she will again stroll through the most beautiful port in the world, and she will walk on Nevi's cliff... When the Moon is almost full and the lights of the seascape project melancholic fireflies on the calm water, you can see her. In the ocean of her memories will remain forever the dark lover who wanted to dance with her, forever alive somewhere, in the realm of princes.

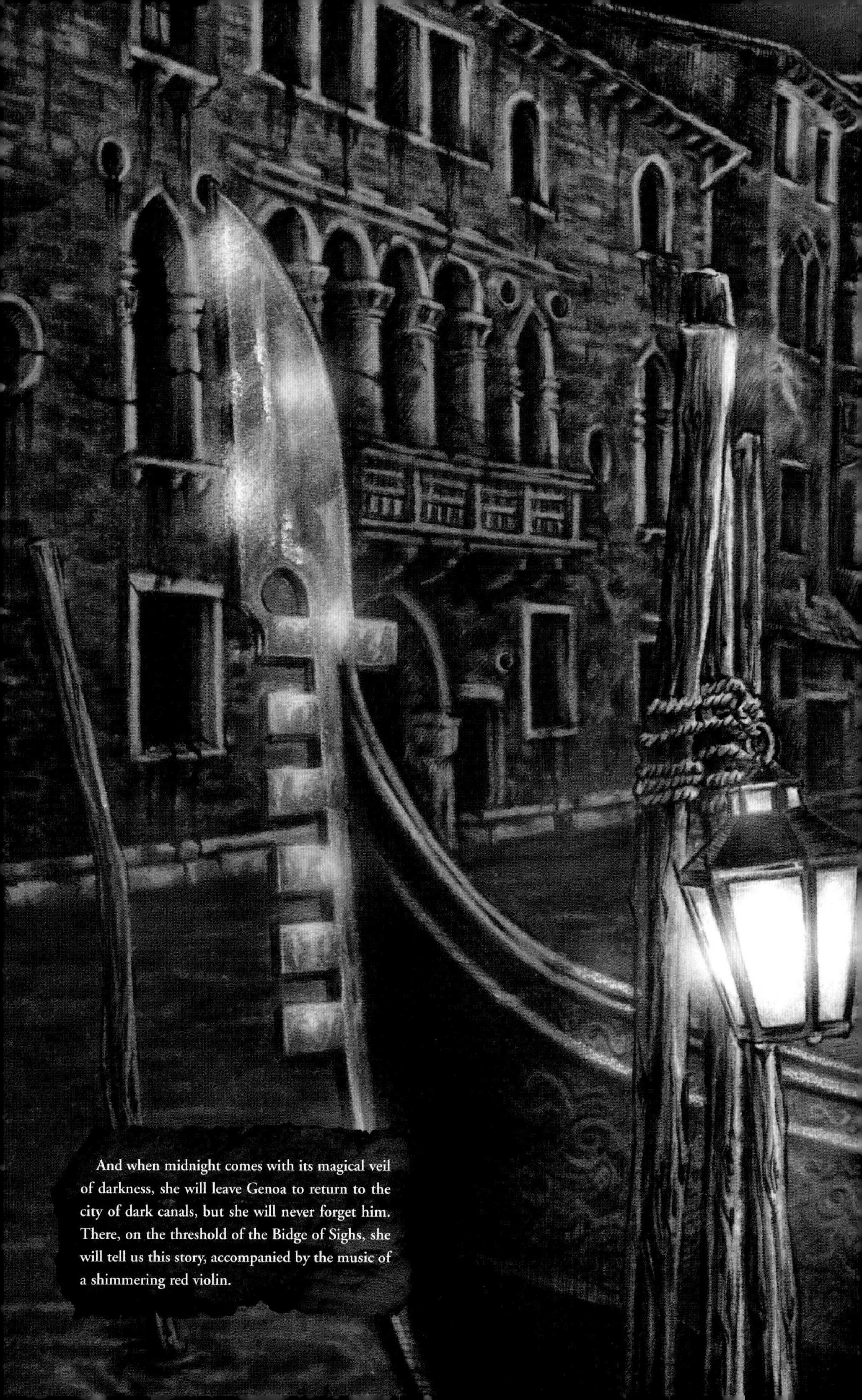

And when midnight comes with its magical veil of darkness, she will leave Genoa to return to the city of dark canals, but she will never forget him. There, on the threshold of the Bidge of Sighs, she will tell us this story, accompanied by the music of a shimmering red violin.

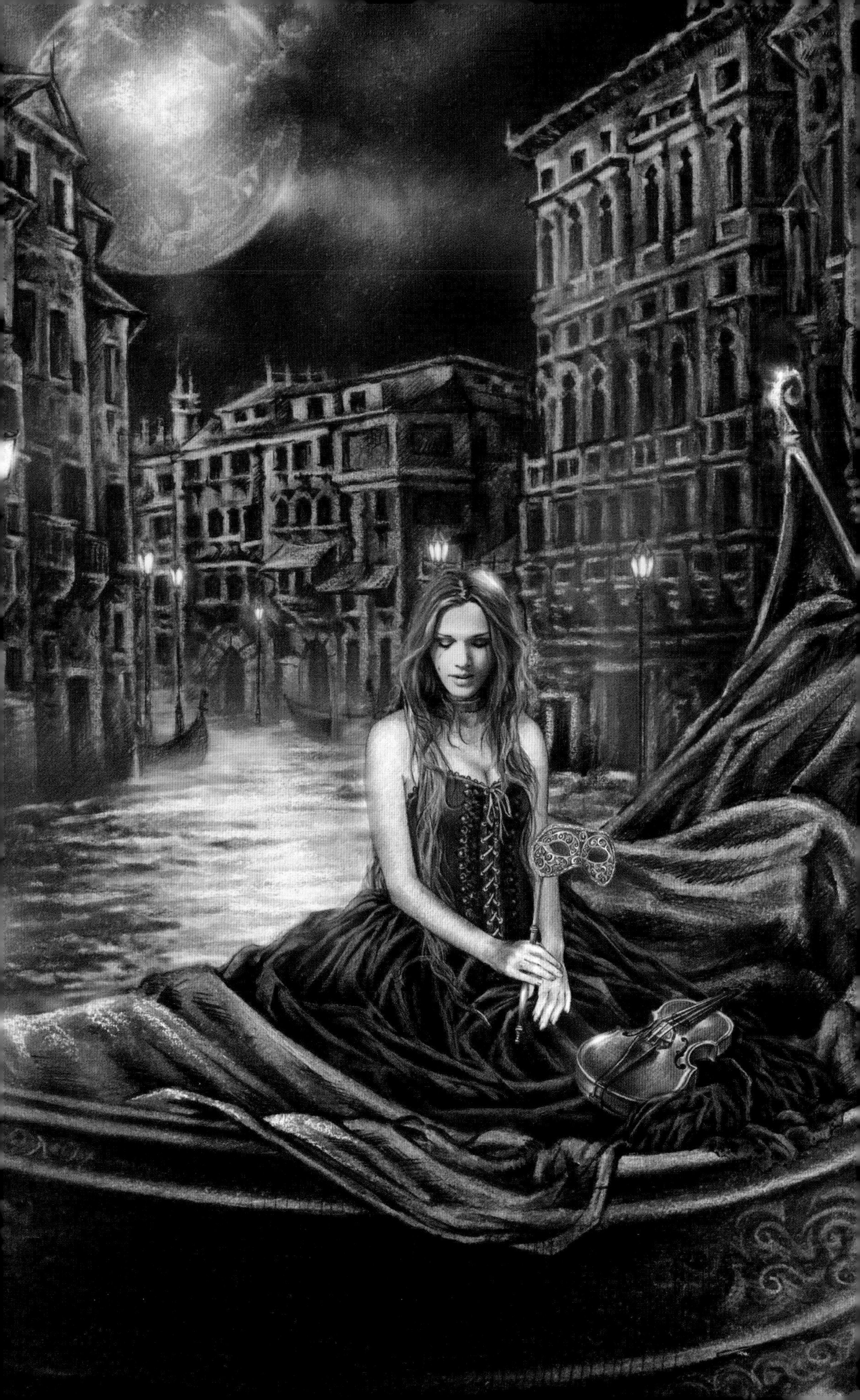

There, in his golden palace, he will discover the beautiful face
he has yearned for...